Ultimate Chinchilla Care

Chinchillas as Pets

The Must Have Guide for Anyone Passionate About Owning a Chinchilla. Includes Health, Toys, Food, Bedding and Lots More…

By Thomas Layton

Foreword

Chinchillas have been increasing in popularity as companion animals since the 1960s. Sadly, from the 1500s forward when they were first encountered by Spanish conquistadores in South America, the beautiful little animals were exploited for their incredibly luxuriant fur.

This practice almost led to their extinction in the wild until a method of "farm raising" them was developed. Still, the largest colony now known to exist in the wild is comprised of only 500 individuals, where once there were groups numbering in the thousands.

As pets, chinchillas are clean and quiet, sleeping most of the day and active in the evening hours. They are strictly indoor animals that spend most of their lives in their cages. If well cared for, they can live for up to 20 years.

They are not, however, suitable pets for young children, and housing them with other pets can be a questionable proposition. Anyone considering acquiring a "chin" must understand that these animals interact with the world from the perspective of prey.

They are timid and nervous in disposition, so care must be taken in captivity to protect them from stress. Even placing their cage at a low angle can lead them to feel they are being "loomed" over. For a small animal often hunted by owls, a large "thing" looking down at them is an instinctive reason for panic.

If, however, you have the patience to sit quietly with your chinchilla and win the little creature's trust, you will be rewarded with the friendship of a bright, inquisitive pet that will chirp happily when you come home at night.

Chinchillas are active and agile, and far too curious for their own good. They need time out of their cages each day, but only in an area that has been rendered "chinchilla proof." They will get themselves into trouble fast, not only because they are avid investigators, but also because they gnaw on everything!

If you think a pet rabbit has the potential to be destructive, you've never met a chinchilla. Keeping a constant supply of safe toys on which your pet can gnaw is essential.

Although chinchillas are subject to gastrointestinal distress if their diets are changed abruptly, their food needs are surprisingly simple – pre-formulated commercial pellets, grass hay, and the occasional treat of fresh fruit and vegetables.

Never purchase a chinchilla – or any pet – as an impulse buy. With this species, you must have all elements of their habitat in place before you bring your new pet home. This will ease the transition for the chinchilla and aid in the animal's adjustment to life as part of your household.

Since your chinchilla will rely on you to provide it with everything it needs to live a happy and healthy life, you have a responsibility to learn all you can about these charming little creatures long before you buy one at a pet store or from a breeder.

This book is intended to help you accomplish this goal, and to make the decision about whether or not a "chin" is the right pet for you. With that in mind, welcome to the world of the chinchilla.

Exclusive Free Offer

Join other chinchilla lovers and owners in our unique **FREE** club – Exclusive to owners of this book.

See page 35 on how to join easily in seconds (and free).

Receive discounts on chinchilla supplies like food and housing. Connect with other members to share knowledge and experience, or ask questions. The best place for lovers of these amazing animals.

Table of Contents

Table of Contents

Chapter 1 – Introduction to Chinchillas

Technically, chinchillas are rodents, but it's impossible to lump these alert and sweet little creatures into any concept you might have of "rat." In fact, there are many qualities that distinguish them from other rodents.

The only other member of the family *Chinchillidae* is the visachas, which is much more rabbit-like in appearance and has highly distinctive orange fur.

If you were casting about for comparisons, chinchillas look like very plump gray squirrels, but with larger heads and

ears. They are part of a specific group of rodents called caviomorphs.

Myomorphs vs. Caviomorphs

The largest group of rodents in the word are the myomorphs, which includes both rats and mice. Chinchillas, and their close relative the guinea pig, are both caviomorphs.

The greatest difference in the two groups is that myomorphs give birth to naked, helpless offspring. Caviomorph young are simply mini copies of their parents. They are born with their eyes open and are immediately active.

Additionally, chinchillas have an unusually long lifespan for a rodent, and can live to 20 years in captivity with good care.

Females have a long gestation period of 111-119 days, and only give birth to a maximum of two litters per year. Rats and mice are much more prolific, and reproduce more frequently.

Although rats, in particular, are known for their cunning cleverness, chinchillas display a complex range of communication skills. When housed near other animals, chinchillas may mimic their sounds, or learn their "language," and respond to them.

Chinchillas also have a great capacity to learn human words and to distinguish their own names from that of a cage mate or other animal in the household.

This ability allows them to be trained with a fair degree of success, and certainly to respond to simple every day commands. It is extremely important, however, never to raise your voice with a chinchilla.

They are sensitive animals that do not like loud noises and they have a long memory. It is quite easy for a chinchilla to decide they don't like someone, but equally difficult to change their minds once that perception is in place.

Two Species of Chinchilla

There are two species of chinchillas. Those that are kept as pets are all believed to be descended from *Chinchilla lanigera,* the long-tailed chinchilla.

These creatures are now found in the wild only on the slopes of the Andes in Chile and on Cordillera de la Costa (the Chilean Coastal Range), which parallels the Andes on the Pacific side of the continent.

Attempts are underway to increase the numbers of long-tailed chinchillas, primarily in a preserve called Las Chinchillas National Reserve.

The short-tailed chinchilla, *Chinchilla brevicaudata,* is even more seriously endangered and is now believed to have gone extinct in the Lauca National Park, a reserve in northern Chile.

As a further limitation on their survival in the wild, chinchillas don't have a very high reproductive rate. (This also accounts for their relatively high cost in the world of pet rodents.)

Chinchillas in History

Chinchillas are indigenous to South America, and are named for the Chincha Indians. The little animals live naturally at altitudes of 16,500 ft (5029 m). They favor rocky outcroppings and cliffs where they can hide in burrows.

When the Spanish first encountered chinchillas in the 1500s, the explorers found groups or colonies that numbered in the thousands.

Before the arrival of the Europeans, the Inca killed chinchillas as a food source, and for their silky, plush pelts, which were turned into opulent royal gowns.

While the Spanish didn't eat the chinchillas, they did adopt the practice of using their fur for royal garments.

Extant records point to a huge demand for chinchilla fur in the 19th century, with 7 million pelts exported from Chile between 1840 and 1916.

The total numbers of the beautiful little animals killed throughout the region in the same period may have been as high as 21 million.

It has been illegal to trap wild chinchilla in Argentina, Bolivia, Chile, and Peru since 1910. From that time forward, there have been concerted efforts to re-establish their presence in the wild.

In the 1920s, when chinchillas were facing complete extinction, an entrepreneur, Mathias F. Chapman, devised a way to breed and "farm" the animals for their fur as a commercial business venture.

While Chapman's efforts did not stop the inhumane exploitation of chinchillas for their fur, it did relieve pressure on the wild population and helped to curb poaching and illegal trapping.

In the 1960s chinchillas began to be kept as pets and to be appreciated for their qualities as companion animals. This fact, coupled with the rising global outcry against the use of animal fur in garments, has greatly improved the chinchilla's lot in the world.

The damage from that barbaric fur trade has still not been repaired, however unrestrained hunting decimated the wild chinchilla population, and due to the species' slow breeding habits, recovery has been modest at best.

Chinchillas, like many animals in South America, also suffer from the effects of habitat destruction. Consequently, the largest chinchilla colony known in the wild today numbers less than 500.

Physical Characteristics

"Wild type" chinchillas are colored in shades of gray to provide maximum camouflage in their preferred rocky environment. Called the "Standard Gray," this type accounts for 90% of the chinchilla population kept as pets around the world.

Thanks to the efforts of breeders, there are numerous color variations, but only one body and coat type. Chinchillas do not exhibit the kinds of size and conformation differences seen in other species like dogs, cats, and rabbits.

Chinchillas have oversized ears and acute hearing to help them detect potential danger, for instance, from the owls that are one of their primary predators. They do not, however, have very good vision, especially during the day.

The best approximation of how a chinchilla sees the world is to compare them to a near-sighted human. Everything at a distance looks like a big blur, and in a chinchilla's prey-centric view of the world, is interpreted as a threat.

Male chinchillas (called bucks) typically weigh 0.8 to 1.1 lbs (0.4 to 0.5 kg), while females (called does) are larger and can reach as much as 1.3 lbs (0.6 kg).

An average individual will measure 9 to 11 inches (23 to 28 cm) in length not including the tail.

Shy by nature, and crepuscular in behavior, chinchillas stay hidden by day, emerging at dusk to start to look for food and not straying far from their burrows.

They use their large whiskers to help them find their way around in the darkness. Like a cat's whiskers, these structures are called vibrissae and are actually sensory organs.

Although their daylight vision is not good, they do have better sight in low light and darkness. Paired with their whiskers, these senses make them highly efficient nocturnal creatures.

In physical conformation, a chinchilla's front legs are very short in contrast to the powerful hindquarters that allow them to hop and jump with great agility.

Since chinchillas can support their full body weight on their back legs, they often "stand up" to get a better view of what's going on around them.

When a "chin" as they are affectionately known by enthusiasts is moving around on all fours, it's a sign that he's happy and relaxed in his surroundings.

The front legs are equipped with tiny little "fingers" that the chinchilla uses to pick up and hold its food and as tools for self-grooming.

Prized for Their Fur

Sadly, these beautiful little creatures have only recently been prized for their gentle and playful personalities. Their incredible, silky fur almost proved to be their undoing.

Until you have petted a chin, it is almost impossible to describe the plushness of their coat, about which they are fastidious in their grooming preferences.

Chinchillas do not bathe in water, nor should you ever get your pet wet. The chapter on daily care will review this process fully, but a chin's favorite way to get clean is a good roll in his dust bath.

Rolling in dust keeps oil and debris out of his luxuriant fur, which is so thick chins are not bothered by parasites such as fleas and ticks.

As a comparison of just how dense a chinchilla's coat really is, humans have only one hair growing from each hair follicle. A chinchilla's follicle will produce up to 80 distinct hairs.

Hypoallergenic?

Although chinchillas are not hypoallergenic per se, their dense fur does not shed dander, which is typically the cause of adverse reactions in sensitive people.

Chinchillas do shed their coats every 3 months or so, but because they groom in dust baths, only occasionally washing their faces, they don't have a concentration of allergy-causing proteins in their fur.

In cats, for instance, the protein Fel d 1 is transferred from the animal's saliva to the fur during grooming. Dried flakes of the protein spread in the environment as dander, triggering an allergic reaction in some people.

Dander is highly species specific, so if you are allergic to cats, you would not necessarily be allergic to any other animal. In general, chinchillas are well-tolerated by people with other pet allergies.

Color Variations

As with any species that gains in popularity as a companion, breeders have, in recent years, begun to expand the available color variations in chinchillas.

(Please note that all prices cited in this book are averages obtained at the time of writing. All currency conversions reflect the then current rate of exchange, and will fluctuate over time.)

Standard

Standard or wild type chinchillas are the typical gray coloration, although some are darker on the upper portions of their body to the point of being "blue."

(Do not confuse a "blue" standard chinchilla with the much rarer "gunmetal" blue now becoming available. A "blue" standard chinchilla is best equated with a very deep gray, while gunmetal chins have a slight purplish hue to their coats. The prices also differ substantially!)

Standard chinchillas tend to be paler on their underparts, and their individual hairs will display alternating bands of dark and light in a patterning called "agouti."

In some chinchillas bred in captivity the banding is missing, however, and the individuals appear to be much darker in coloration.

Standard gray chinchillas are easy to find, and typically cost $75 / £46 per individual.

White or Pale

There are a number of white chinchillas that first appeared in the 1950s. One of the most prominent of these is Wilson's White.

These chinchillas are not albinos, exhibiting dark rather than pink ears and black eyes. (Real albinos have red eyes.)

The "pink white" chinchilla, although a close match to an albino, does retain some pigment, which can be seen in faint beige "veiling" or tipping.

White chinchillas are most readily available from breeders, and cost $150 to $200 / £93 to £124.

Mosaic or Pied

Although these chinchillas are often predominately white, they also have patches of dark fur. Their patterning is completely unpredictable, and unique per individual.

The pattern does breed true, however, but can be widely varied even in a single litter. For many enthusiasts, this variability is what makes mosaic chinchillas so interesting.

These colorations are rarely available in pet stores. From a breeder, you will pay approximately $150 / £93 per chinchilla.

Beige Shades

The champagne shade has become highly popular in recent years. These chins are especially handsome because their underparts are white.

The depth of the beige coloring will vary from relatively dark to a beautiful cream. One of the most popular of these is the Willman's Beige.

You may see these chinchillas described as "pearls" or "pastels" depending on their coloring.

Depending on the depth of the beige coloration, and the availability from breeders, these chins will cost $150 to $300 / £93 to £186.

Blacks and Browns

Breeders developed the "black velvet" in 1956, a sleek, jet black chinchilla with a white belly. Now, there is also a grayer variation known as a "charcoal," which is occasionally referred to as an "ebony."

The brown velvet also has a white underbelly, as opposed to the ordinary brown, which is less intense after the fashion of the charcoal.

Black and brown colorations are becoming more popular and easier to find. On average, individuals in these shades cost $150 to $200 / £93 to £124. Some charcoals, however, sell for as much as $500 / £310.

Violet

Currently, the rarest and most unusual mutation is the violet. This coloration was cultivated by controlled breeding programs in Zimbabwe, with the result being a "pointed" animal.

The best comparison of any animal with points is to a Siamese cat. The chin's extremities (face, feet, and tail) are darker than its body, which is a purplish soft gray.

Violet chinchillas are very hard to find, and will cost anywhere from $200 to $400 / £124 to £247 depending on the quality of the coloration.

Rare Colorations

The range of colorations in chinchillas continues to evolve, especially as the animals are beginning to be judged more commonly in breeder shows.

These venues are not competitions, per se, but settings where chinchillas are rated in quality against an accepted breed standard.

For this reason, and for the profitability to be had from selling chinchillas as pets, breeders have a vested interest in improving their bloodlines, and in developing new varieties.

Often breeders will display new and unique mutations at shows like the "sapphire," which is best described as "gunmetal" blue in color with white underparts.

Sapphire chinchillas sell in the $250 to $300 / £155 to £186 price range, while the even rarer blues may cost as much as $500 / £310.

Interestingly, there appears to be absolutely no difference in temperament with any of the color mutations. Chinchillas are amazingly consistent in their behavior and demeanor.

Suitability as Pets

Chinchillas make attractive pets because they are easily housed in small homes including apartments. They do have generally nervous dispositions, and they don't like loud noises, startling easily.

Realize that in adopting any animal, you have a responsibility to appreciate the creature for who and what it is, not for what you think you can make of it.

A chinchilla interacts with its environment from its own unique perspective. While a chin will get used to your home and to you, you can't ask it to just stop being a chinchilla, nor should you even try.

Although it takes some initial patience to get to know a chinchilla, they do bond well with their humans – like glue, in fact.

Chinchillas pick one person to whom they give their full devotion. They may spend two or three months making up their minds, but then you will have a friend for life.

Individual chins vary in the degree to which they enjoy being held, but all chinchillas like to be petted, generally approaching you on their own terms.

They are quiet animals, although they do have extensive abilities to communicate. Typically, chinchillas don't like strangers, and will retreat into their nest box or a corner and watch what's going on with typical chin wariness.

Chins like routine, so much so that after a few months, you'll think your pet wears a wristwatch. He'll want you to do everything the same way, at the same time, every day.

That's a small thing to give to a pet that offers such benefits as no unpleasant odor, requires a fairly predictable amount of space, and sleeps happily all day in his cage while you're at work.

A chinchilla's dietary requirements are simple, consisting mainly of specially formulated food pellets and hay. They do, however, have very sensitive digestive systems and do not tolerate abrupt changes in their food supply.

If you think I sound like a broken record, prepare for this song to play several times -- chinchillas have a long lifespan of 15-20 years with good care.

For most owners this is seen as an advantage, but if you are not prepared to give a chinchilla the care it needs for a long period of time, don't adopt one.

No matter how cute you think that chin is in the moment, you must consider the long-term commitment to a living animal you are undertaking and be serious about what you are doing.

All pets deserve excellent long-term care and attention, but it's important to understand exactly what "long" means before you adopt.

Think before you buy!

Strictly Indoor Pets

Chinchillas are strictly indoor pets. They can get away from you fast, and once they are on their own, they will easily fall prey to the first predator they encounter.

Additionally, chinchillas are very heat sensitive and must be carefully protected from any potential of heatstroke. They do best at an average temperature of 75° F / 24° C.

Chinchillas and Children?

Chinchillas are only suitable as pets for older children, with supervision. Children younger than seven years of age will be able to help care for a chinchilla, but they will not be able to manage all of the chores on their own, and they may not understand the sensitive nature of these creatures.

This sensitivity is a matter of both temperament and physiology. A chinchilla's bone structure is fragile. The bones are light and break easily. Many experts liken handling a chinchilla to holding a bird. The same degree of care is required at all times.

Chinchillas rarely bite if handled appropriately. They are, by nature, more timid than aggressive. In the early stages of getting to know an individual, you don't want to waggle your finger in the cage, however. The chin might mistake it for a treat.

It should always be stressed to children and adults alike that you should never yell at a chinchilla, or menace it in any way in its habitat — including tapping on the bars or shaking the cage.

Chinchillas need to feel safe and secure in their enclosures, and they are easily intimidated and frightened. This is even a consideration in cage placement. Never "loom" over a chinchilla. Always place its cage at chest level so you are meeting the little creature face to face.

It is also imperative that children understand that chinchillas must never be left out of their cage unattended. Chins are insatiably curious and given to chewing. They get themselves into trouble fast.

Chinchillas and Other Pets

Always remember your chinchilla's place in the food chain. They stay close to their burrows in the wild for good reason. Many larger animals want to eat them!

If you have other pets, keep them away from your chinchilla. This is especially important in the case of cats. Fluffy doesn't have to be able to get to your chin to do it serious harm.

Imagine how you would feel if you were a chinchilla having to look up at a cat sitting on top of your cage perhaps taking paw swipes down into your world.

While dogs will generally ignore a chinchilla in its cage, don't let Fido and your chin loose in the same room. Your dog's native hunting instincts might take over, or he might mistake the chinchilla for a toy and injure it severely.

Both ferrets and rats are native predators. They should never be allowed to interact with chinchillas, even if the chins are safely inside their cages. If the chinchilla is not physically injured, it will become seriously agitated.

Chinchillas are sensitive creatures. Their sense of caution and fear serves them well in the wild, keeping them constantly alert to potential danger.

In their homes, however, they feel secure, which is exactly how you want them to feel in the home you will share with them.

Bottom line - chinchillas and other pets don't mix.

Any Bad Habits?

Chinchillas engage in two defensive behaviors that can be technically classified as "bad" habits, although again, this is just an instance of a chinchilla being a chinchilla.

Spraying

If you have male chinchillas, and they are presented with a newcomer, or any other reason to express territorial displeasure, they can spray.

Essentially, your pet will stand up and let fly with a stream of very strong smelling urine. This is absolutely one of those times when, no matter how much you may want to, yelling at your chinchilla will do nothing but frighten him and make the situation worse.

As much as I hate to resort to the trite "boys will be boys," it's the truth in regard to spraying behavior. If you are concerned about this potential, the answer it quite simple — keep female chinchillas!

It's also only fair to point out, however, that if sufficiently upset, female chinchillas will spray as well, while some males will just stand up and chatter vehemently to express their displeasure.

Nature has not equipped the chinchilla with many defense mechanisms, so they use what they have, including spraying. This is not, however, a completely predictable behavior.

Typically unless chinchillas are really angry or threatened, spraying is not an issue.

Fur Blowing

Chinchillas have the ability to essentially turn loose of their fur to get away. They do this when they are startled or frightened. One minute you're holding a chinchilla, and the next you're covered in chinchilla fur.

While this is disconcerting for owners, the thing you should be most concerned about it not letting your chin get scared or nervous enough to blow its fur in the first place.

The effect of the incident on the fur is not long term. Chins have plenty of hair, and what they lose will grow back. Instead, look to and correct the source of the stress or alarm, including altering your own behavior.

Never try to grab at or tightly restrain a chinchilla that is trying to struggle to get away from you. You can injure your pet severely, and you'll certainly wind up with a mountain of loose fur all over you and everything near you.

Male or Female

There really is very little difference in disposition between male and female chinchillas. Both make excellent pets. If, however, you are ultimately planning on keeping a pair of chins, it's best to start with a female.

Males that have lived alone tend to be less receptive to being presented with a "roomie" later in life, and can be quite aggressive, especially to other males even in the absence of a female.

It's hard to believe looking at these adorable little creatures, but they can and do fight when there's a dispute in chinchillaland, with torn ears and other abrasions generally the result.

Chins have very sharp teeth, and although they will rarely use them on you, their fights with one another tend to be no holds barred.

One or Two?

Chinchillas are highly social. If you have the space, and can make the time commitment, a pair of chinchillas will be quite happy together.

Since they sleep by day, even a single chin will do well while you're at work, waking up about the time you come home at the end of the day.

Still, the companionship of another creature of their own kind is very comforting to chinchillas because they live in colonies in the wild. Two chins playing together is a rare sight. They do know how to have fun!

If you do decide to keep two chinchillas, acquire your pets at the same time if at all possible. In general, it's much easier to keep pairs of female chinchillas since males can be aggressively territorial.

Summary of Chinchilla Characteristics

- Odor free.
- Clean to the point of fastidiousness.
- Not troubled by fleas or ticks.
- No dander, so well tolerated by people with allergies.
- Quiet, with a tendency to be shy.
- Don't like loud noises and are easily startled.
- Sleep during the day.
- Social, but they have to get used to you.
- Rarely bite.
- Tame if handled consistently from an early age.
- Exclusively indoor pets.
- Should not be allowed to roam free.
- Will chew vigorously.
- Need an average temperature of 75° F / 24° C.
- Must be carefully protected from heatstroke.
- Lifespan of 15-20 years.

Exclusive FREE Offer – How to Join

Join other Chinchilla lovers in our unique **FREE** club – Exclusive to owners of this book.

It's quick and easy to sign up. You can receive discounts on chinchilla food, supplies and more including connecting with other owners. Here's how in 2 simple steps…

Step 1

Go to http://www.ChinchillaBook.com
Enter your name and email address and click 'Join.'

Step 2

Confirm your subscription. As soon as you sign up we'll send you an email asking you to confirm the details are correct. Just click the link in the email and you'll be joined free.

If you don't receive the email please check your spam folder and that you used the correct email address.

It's as easy as that. Any questions please email support@chinchillabook.com and where possible we will help.

Chapter 2 – Buying a Chinchilla

After reading Chapter 1, you will hopefully have a basic understanding of a chinchilla's personality and suitability as a pet before you make a decision to buy one.

Please do not immediately go out and acquire a chin without reading Chapter 4 on daily care, however. One of the most important things to know about chinchillas – before you buy one – is their nervous disposition.

It is absolutely essential to a successful transition that you have your pet's environment completely established before you bring the chin home.

You want to be able to gently and quietly remove the chin from its carrier, put it in its new habitat, and leave it alone to get used to its changed surroundings.

The less you subject a chinchilla to jarring changes – including changes in its diet, the better your new pet will adapt and the sooner it will bond with you.

Also remember these key points that were covered in Chapter 1:

- Chinchillas do not like loud noises.
- They are not appropriate pets for young children.
- Chins must be kept isolated from other pets.
- A chinchilla is an exclusively indoor pet.
- They will chew everything, so don't leave them unattended.
- They need an average temperature of 75° F / 24° C.
- Chinchillas have an expected lifespan of 15-20 years.

Picking a Chinchilla

It's now quite simple to find a chinchilla to adopt in a pet store. Most of these chins are "wild" or "standard" grays. If you are interested in unusual colors, you will probably need to locate a breeder.

Never bring a chinchilla home that is younger than 16 weeks. It should be fully weaned, and preferably used to being handled.

Note, however, that even with a well-socialized young chinchilla there will still be a period of "taming" while the animal gets used to you.

One of the most important things to understand about living with a pet chinchilla is that they interact with the world from the perspective of "prey." You must take precautions to make sure your chin feels secure and protected in its new environment.

If you are adopting a fully grown chinchilla, it's practically impossible to determine their age, so you'll have to go on the word of the pet store owner or breeder.

Other things to look for in evaluating a chinchilla for adoption include:

- Firm, dry droppings in its enclosure with no sign of diarrhea.

- A bright, alert, and active demeanor, especially in young individuals.

- Plush, soft fur that stands erect with good texture.

- Bright eyes with no sign of tears or discharge.

- Upright, clean ears free of debris with no evidence of tears or rips.

- No discharge from the nose, sniffling, or sneezing.

Gently pull down the fur around the mouth so you can look at the lower incisors, and lift the skin on the upper "lip" to examine the top teeth.

The teeth should be intact and meet normally, which will indicate that the chin will be able to eat properly. If the teeth do not meet, the chinchilla is suffering from a condition called a dental malocclusion.

A chinchilla with a malocculsion can certainly be adopted, and will be a good pet, but its teeth will have to be trimmed back regularly, generally at two-month intervals.

Most owners prefer not to attempt dental trimming on their own, so if you adopt a pet with a dental malocculsion you must have access to an exotic animal veterinarian. This will mean an added expense in the care of your chinchilla.

Choose Based on Personality

It's always best to make your final choice based on personality rather than gender or coloration. In most cases you want to visit a breeder's facility in the early evening when the chins are just waking up.

Let the breeder interact with the chinchillas while you watch from a distance. Hopefully you will be able to observe a set of parents and their young.

Watching the older animals will give you some indication of how the juveniles will probably mature. (Watching the breeder will show you how the little animals have been socialized.)

Be assured, however, that chinchillas have very distinct and individual personalities, and their own set of likes and dislikes, including their opinions about people.

Chinchillas are also, however, extremely curious by nature. Ultimately, one will decide to come check you out because something about you has intrigued the chin.

That's a good foundation on which to start building a long-term relationship.

Remember, there is no difference in behavior and temperament by gender or color variation, but all chinchillas have distinct personalities. You're always going to do better when you are your chinchilla's first choice.

Determining Gender

Once a chinchilla is fully grown, it is virtually impossible to determine the age of an individual. Sexing a chinchilla is somewhat easier.

When examined from the underside, the spacing between the two orifices located near the base of the tail indicates gender. This is called the "ano-genital gap."

In females, the space is short, but much longer in males. After a male has attained three months of age, his testes will appear in the gap as evident swellings.

When chinchillas are fully grown, it's easier to distinguish males and females in a group. The males are smaller than the females in body size, but their heads are larger.

Buying at a Pet Store

When buying from a pet store, you will do better to find one that is not actively displaying their chinchillas for the scrutiny of customers. Chinchillas are nocturnal and shy, so being on general display is very stressful for them.

Ask to examine the living conditions to make sure that none of the individuals are showing signs of illness, including diarrhea, which is potentially serious in chins. All droppings in the enclosure should by dry and firm.

If the pet store refuses to allow you to handle the chinchilla or otherwise to verify its health, move on. Also, do not believe a store's determination of gender. Most of the time they make the wrong call!

Working with a Breeder

Buying from a respected breeder is always your best option, especially if you are interested in a specific color mutation. Breeders are typically not only happy, but enthusiastic to show off their animals and to talk about their operation.

When you buy from a breeder, you will be ensuring that you have a source of back-up information and advice. In the best of all possible worlds, you'll stay in touch with your breeder.

Hopefully, that person will help you learn how to care for your new pet and ensure continuity in the chin's transition to your home.

This is absolutely essential in terms of diet. As you'll see in Chapter 4, chinchillas are highly susceptible to digestive upset and it's important to introduce any changes gradually and carefully.

A chinchilla going to a new home should always receive whatever diet it has become accustomed to receiving during the first months of its life.

When working with a breeder, expect to answer as many — or more — questions as you will ask. (Sometimes you may even be asked to fill out a questionnaire!)

A breeder should care about the animals they are selling and be anxious to know they are going to a good home. This is a sign of a dedicated enthusiast and very much a "positive."

Chinchilla Rescues

It is all too common for chinchillas to be surrendered to rescue organizations for any one of a number of reasons. People's life circumstances change, they underestimated the amount of care the chin needed, or there was an unexpected litter.

Please consider checking with a rescue organization and taking in one of these orphaned chinchillas when you are thinking of acquiring a chin for a pet. These animals are in desperate need of homes.

On the other side of the equation, however, if you are in a position to surrender a chinchilla, please verify the legitimacy of the rescue organization you are considering.

There is always a chance that an animal hoarder may pose as a rescuer and you will unwittingly give your pet over to someone who will neither care for it appropriately, nor attempt to place it in a new home.

If you are adopting from a rescue group, understand that the chinchilla you bring home may need extra love, attention, and patience.

Chins coming from a rescue environment acclimate slowly to their new surroundings. In the end, however, you are not just bringing home a pet, but very likely saving a life.

(Please refer to the back of this book for a listing of chinchilla rescue groups.)

Pros and Cons of Ownership

What one person might regard as a "pro" of chinchilla ownership another might see as a "con." Only you can decide, but these are certainly key points to remember:

- There is a danger of buying a chinchilla on impulse because they are so exquisitely soft and plush. Don't do it! This is a sensitive species that requires foreknowledge on the part of the buyer.

- Chinchillas are not necessarily "high maintenance," but they do have specific needs that must be met. Please read Chapter 4 on daily care carefully before you purchase a chin.

- These are very active agile, animals. They do require time outside of their cages in the evening.

- Because chinchillas are rodents with a need to keep their teeth worn down, you must "chinchilla proof" at least one room in your house. Never let a chinchilla roam around unsupervised, however. They're very inquisitive and prone to get into trouble.

- Chinchillas do require facilities to take dust baths, which can create quite a mess for you to clean up. Never bathe a chinchilla in water, however.

- Because the lush fur of a chinchilla does not produce dander, they are generally well tolerated by people with allergies.

- If you are going to keep a pair, pick females. Males can show territorial aggression that can include the spraying of pungent urine.

- Chinchillas are not appropriate pets for young children.

- This species requires tall, multi-level cages with sleeping boxes and lots of places to hide.

- The captive lifespan of a well-cared-for chinchilla is 15-20 years.

How Much Does a Chinchilla Cost?

Although prices will be different depending on where you buy your pet, it is possible to get a general idea of what it will cost you to purchase a chinchilla according to color variation.

(Please note that the following prices were averages at the time of this writing, and that all currency conversions are subject to fluctuation.)

Standard Gray
$75 / £46

White or Pale
$150-$200 / £93-£124

Mosaic or Pied
$150 / £93

Beige Shades
$150-$300 / £93-£186

Blacks and Browns
$150-$200 / £93-£124

Charcoals
up to $500 / £310

Violet
$200-$400 / £124-£247

Sapphire
$250-$300 / £155-£186

Gunmetal Blue
$500 / £310

A Word About Buying in Pairs

Breeders will often offer a lower price when chinchillas are sold in pairs. If you're a bargain shopper, think twice . . . and then twice again.

Don't make the decision to adopt a pair of chinchillas based on price alone!

Chinchillas are herd animals, and they do enjoy having a cage mate, but you will need twice the space, twice the equipment, and twice the commitment!

Remember that you are considering adopting a companion animal that can live as long as 20 years. Do not make that step lightly for a single chinchilla, much less for two.

If you do decide to buy a pair, and as long as the animals know one another and are established in an environment at the same time, same gender cage mates should get along well.

Males can be territorial, however, so especially for a first-time chinchilla owner, going with two females is likely the better option.

Pet Stores Get It Wrong!

Pet stores are notorious for failing to sex chinchillas correctly, which accounts for most of the unwanted litters born in the homes of trusting customers each year.

If you know from the beginning that you want a pair of chinchillas, work with a breeder. Absolutely establishing gender before housing chins together is imperative to avoid unwanted litters.

There are far too many chins in rescue situations already. Don't contribute to the problem, even unwittingly. Responsible chin ownership starts from day one!

Chapter 3 – Designing a Habitat

Because chinchillas are sensitive to changes in their environment, it's extremely important to have their habitat completely set up before you bring your new pet home.

This is especially crucial in regard to diet to avoid dangerous digestive upset. Talk to your breeder or to the pet store and find out exactly what the chinchilla has been eating. Do not deviate from this diet in the beginning.

Since an established habitat is so crucial, the first stage of chinchilla ownership is putting together a shopping list.

Shopping for Your Chinchilla

The following items are the absolute essentials on your shopping list to create a habitat for your chin.

Bear in mind that while most of these items are available at your local pet store (especially if it's of the "big box" sort), you may have to engineer other aspects of your chin's home on your own.

- Cage / habitat
- Nest box
- Bedding
- Litter scoop
- Food bowl
- Hay rack

- Exercise wheel
- Dust bath
- Stainless steel comb
- Small pet carrier

The next chapter will discuss food for your pet, with estimated costs. I cannot stress strongly enough – or often enough – that in the beginning, you must feed your chin whatever it is used to eating to avoid digestive upset.

If you want to change or improve your pet's diet, this must be done very gradually over a period of several weeks, by slowly decreasing the amount of the old diet while adding the new pellets or hay. Any other approach is an invitation for trouble.

Cage

With any species of pet that lives primarily in a cage, the standard rule of habitat purchasing is always the same: buy the biggest cage you can afford and that can be placed in your home. Chinchillas are active and they need a fair amount of space.

The absolute minimum recommended size for a chinchilla enclosure is 2 ft x 2 ft / 0.6 m x 0.6 m. Bigger is better, and think "up" instead of "out."

Chins like to climb and jump. Their home in captivity needs to be their "cliff," complete with perches, solid ramps, and lots of places to hide.

Remember, chins have a fragile skeletal structure and can break bones easily. Make sure there are no places where they can catch their feet and injure themselves.

Keep an eye toward safe materials. Chinchillas will literally destroy plastic, which can be a choking hazard and certainly a potentially toxic substance.

Go with non-coated stainless steel, and opt for a solid floor, or a floor that has an extensive amount of solid space.

While a tray to catch droppings through mesh is convenient for you, it can be very painful for your pet and potentially harmful if the animal's feet slip through the holes.

Recommended sizes for the wire mesh on a chin's cage are:

- 1 in x 0.5 in (2.54 cm x 1.27 cm) on the sides
- 0.5 in x 0.5 in (1.27 cm x 1.27 cm) on the floor

Also opt for a cage with a door large enough to allow you to easily reach inside and remove your pet with plenty of clearance. For this reason, many bird cages, though tall enough, are completely inappropriate for chins because the doors are too small.

Small animal cages designed for creatures like chinchillas, ferrets or guinea pigs are typically available in a range of prices from about $175-$350 / £110-£220 depending on size, complexity, and number of included amenities like perches and solid ramps.

You can see a selection of good cages here
http://www.ChinchillaBook.com/cages.htm (USA)
http://www.ChinchillaBook.com/cagesuk.htm (UK)

Option for an Open Pen

If you have a closet, or a corner of a room that can be dedicated to a permanent play area, it's possible to use wire panels to create an indoor "fence."

All of the same safety considerations for materials and mesh size should apply to selecting or having the panels fabricated.

This can be a good alternative to permanently chinchilla proof an entire room, but your panels will need to be 6 feet tall / 1.8 meters or higher. Chinchillas are excellent jumpers. Don't underestimate them.

Cage Placement

Optimum cage placement will allow you to interact with your chinchilla while allowing the little creature to feel safe.

Choose a Corner

Never put a chin's cage out in the center of the room. Remember that in the wild, they live on rocky cliffs. If you have an available corner that will make your pet feel protected on two sides, this is ideal.

Chins like to be able to feel that they are retreating with a secure wall against their backs to observe what's going on. Corners make them feel much less exposed in their environment.

Position at Chest Level

Also, place the cage at roughly chest level so you are not "looming" over your chin when you approach its habitat.

Always remember that chinchillas see the world from the perspective of prey. A big creature coming at him from above isn't going to make a chinchilla happy!

(Placing the cage higher off the ground will also protect your chin from being frightened by other pets in the house. Never let a cat sit on top of your chin's cage. The level of anxiety this will cause the chinchilla can be life threatening.)

Over the course of the first few weeks, your chin will come to know and trust you, but cage placement and arrangement is an important part in this taming and socialization process.

Avoid Heat Sources

Also, chinchillas are susceptible to heat stroke, so do not place their cage in front of a window or near any type of heat source.

You are striving for an optimum temperature of 75° F / 24° C. Use a thermometer. Don't guess. Overheating is a leading cause of death for pet chinchillas.

If you see your chin stretched out rather than "hunched" up, the little animal is too hot and is trying to cool itself down. This, coupled with labored breathing is a sure sign of distress that must be relieved.

Any time your chinchilla has become overheated, immediately remove your pet to a cooler area, but don't subject him to drafts. A fan in the room will help, but don't point it right at your chin.

Watch the Humidity

You will also want to keep an eye on the humidity in the room where you position your chinchilla's habitat. The optimum range for the condition of their coats is 30-40% humidity.

A bathroom is a great place for a chin to play with supervision, for instance, but not as a location for their habitat. In most homes the bathroom is the most humid room in the house.

High humidity will also increase the risk of heat stroke, so monitor this reading especially during the summer months.

Consider Lighting and Sound

While you do not want to subject your chinchillas to direct sunlight, they do like a 12-hour light/dark cycle. The only difference is that they like to be out and about while it's dark.

During the day, while you're at work, make sure their room is comfortably dim. If the light bothers them, they'll go into their nest box. It's not uncommon to come home, however, and find a sleepy chin sacked out on one of his perches.

(If your chin has a favorite perch for snoozing, consider covering the cage behind that spot with heavy cardboard to make it more like a "cave.")

They have a tendency to fall asleep in funny positions because they get so groggy during the day, sometimes even leaning up against a cage feature while standing on their hind legs.

At night, however, they will be most active and they enjoy having some sound in the room. Leave a radio on for your pets, and don't be surprised if you sneak a peak and find them up on their hind legs "dancing."

Chin owners report that their pets have favorite songs and respond enthusiastically when they hear them. They've also been known to actively watch television.

Note that if you have to be away for the weekend, it's important for the house not to be completely silent.

Chinchillas don't like loud noises, but conversely, they get nervous when things are too quiet and all the normal sounds are gone.

Position Away from Kitchen

Don't place your chinchilla's cage near the kitchen. Many cooking appliances and implements, especially those that have a non-stick surface, can give off toxic fumes, particularly at high temperatures.

While those chemicals in the air aren't necessarily sufficient to harm you, they can be deadly to your pet. These reactions can occur very rapidly, and your pet can be in extreme distress before you realize anything is wrong.

Don't Choose a Bedroom

Finally, since chinchillas are most active at night, it's best not to put their cage in anyone's bedroom — especially if they have an exercise wheel that doesn't run smoothly!

Chinchillas are also smart and they like to have their own way. If they know you're in the same room and they want some attention, they're quite capable of making enough noise to get you up – all with a perfectly innocent expression on their sweet little faces.

Nest Box

For a pet chinchilla, the nest box is the equivalent of its burrow or cave. Don't put this box on the floor of the enclosure, but on a platform higher up in the cage.

The box should be large enough for the chinchilla to stand (on all fours) and turn around easily. If you have two chinchillas, the box should have room for both. The back of the box should be open for ventilation and cleaning.

A variety of commercially produced nest boxes are available starting at $30 / £19 and up. These may be made of anything from wood to galvanized steel.

Typically these units offer some means of attachment so they can be secured to the side of the cage. It's actually best for the nest box to be replaceable; it's highly likely your chin will gnaw on the corners.

It's certainly possible to construct your own nest box, just observe all the applicable precautions about materials, including using wood that has not been treated in any way.

If you'd like to see a selection of nest boxes please look at:
http://www.ChinchillaBook.com/nestbox.htm (USA)
http://www.ChinchillaBook.com/nextboxuk.htm (UK)

Hiding Spots and Branches

Since chinchillas like multiple hiding spaces, you can also use things like lengths of clay pipe on the floor of the enclosure to give them places to dart into at a second's notice. Chins will actually be more forthcoming in their habits if they know they can dash to "safety" in an instant.

Chinchillas enjoy branches for climbing and chewing. These should be cut from trees that have not come into contact with any insecticides or chemicals.

Do not use branches from cherry, yew, or laburnum trees as these will be toxic to your pet. Good choices are apple or sycamore.

Bedding

The most commonly used bedding material for the base of a chinchilla's care is some sort of wood shavings, preferably aspen, which is considered the safest.
Do not use either cedar or pine shavings as both contain phenols that are potentially toxic to chinchillas.

Line the bottom of the enclosure with about 1 in / 2.5 cm of shavings. Use the kind of scoop typically used with cats' litter boxes to remove soiled bedding and droppings on a daily basis.

Two cubic feet / 56.6 liters of aspen bedding sells for approximately $15 / £9, while a litter scoop will cost $5-$10 / £3-£6.

You should see some good deals here:
http://www.ChinchillaBook.com/bedding.htm (USA)

Note on Litter "Training"

Chinchillas cannot be litter trained. You will need to remove droppings from their enclosure daily, and there will be "accidents" when they are outside of their habitat.

Fortunately, their urinary output is extremely small, and their pellets should be dry and firm. As an added plus, chins tend to pick one corner or spot in their cage where they will urinate.

If you let them have free time in the same room where their habitat is located, and leave the cage door open, they will often go back inside to "use the bathroom."

If not, however, they will typically not urinate outside the cage and can go for as long as two hours without any accidents.

Even in their play area, they may pick a favorite location to urinate, which will allow you to anticipate their behavior and protect the flooring in some way.

(If you are keeping more than one chin, the spot won't be the same – inside the cage or out. Each animal will choose its own corner, and expect their "rights" to be respected!)

Unfortunately, chinchillas do not have the same habitual response to dropping pellets. That will happen pretty much where ever they are, and the output can be fairly steady.

Take it as a plus, however, that if your chin gets away and is hiding from you, you can just follow the trail he obligingly leaves behind!

All in all, however, cleaning up after your chin is highly manageable, even more so if your pet's free time is in a room with a hardwood or tiled floor as opposed to carpet or rugs.

Food and Water Containers

The best choices for food bowls to be used with chinchillas are heavy ceramic or earthenware models. Plastic is too light, and your chins will just chew it up. You can also opt for stainless steel bowls that can be affixed to the side of the habitat.

Expect to pay $20-$30 / £13-£19 for earthenware and $10-$15 / £6-£9 for stainless steel.
Water bottles with stainless, ball bearing "lixit" tips are the most efficient option with chinchillas. Be sure to place the spout at the same level as your pet's mouth for ease of access.

A 16-ounce / 0.47 liter water bottle will cost $18-$20 / £11-£13.

You can see some bowls and food containers at:
http://www.ChinchillaBook.com/bowl.htm (USA)
http://www.ChinchillaBook.com/bowluk.htm (UK)

Hay Rack

Hay is an integral part of a chinchilla's diet, but it should never be scattered on the floor of the enclosure where it will become mixed in with the bedding and fouled.

Invest in a small hay rack that will attach to the side of the cage, which will cost approximately $8 / £5.

http://www.ChinchillaBook.com/hay.htm (USA)
http://www.ChinchillaBook.com/hayuk.htm (UK)

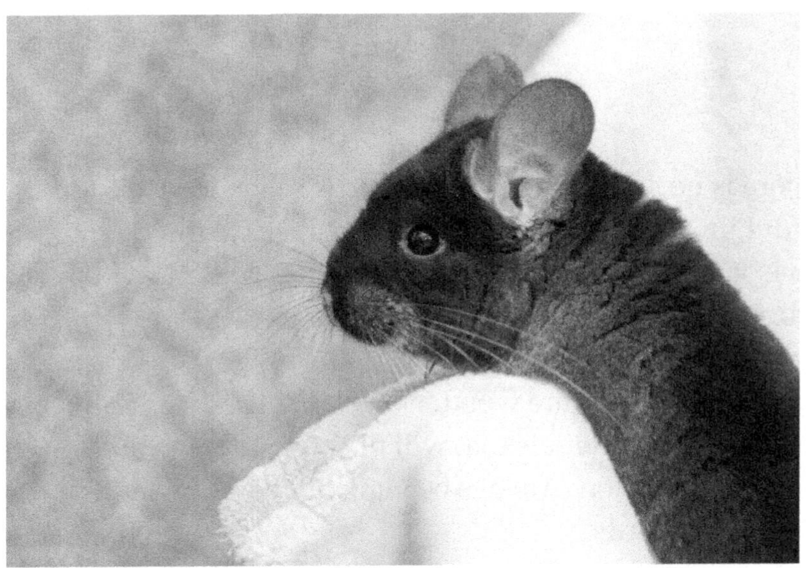

Exercise Wheel

Exercise wheels are a great way for your chinchilla to burn off energy and cover a lot of "distance" without ever leaving his habitat. Be sure to find a totally enclosed unit with no gaps between the rungs.

Place it snuggly up against the side of the cage allowing for no gaps in which your pet's tail can become caught and be injured.

To purchase an exercise wheel large enough for a chinchilla, expect to spend $25-$30 / £16-£19.

Need an exercise wheel? You could try:
http://www.ChinchillaBook.com/wheel.htm (USA)
http://www.ChinchillaBook.com/wheeluk.htm (UK)

Chew Toys

There is no such thing as "too much" when it comes to providing chew toys for a pet chinchilla. Their four sharp incisor teeth grow throughout their lives and must be kept worn down through vigorous gnawing.

Your best options are wooden blocks, since other chew toys may contain materials that will upset your chinchilla's delicate digestion. Always be vigilant about potential choking hazards.

Often sold in lots of 6-12 pieces, wooden blocks for your chinchilla will cost approximately $12.50-$25 / £8-£16.

They will also enjoy heavy cardboard tubes, using them as chewing toys and as tunnels for running and hiding. Also look into "Roll-a-Nest" balls made by Super Pet.

These items come in various sizes. They are made of safe sisal and have openings for your chinchillas to duck inside and hide. In a size large enough for a chinchilla, a Roll-a-Nest costs approximately $15 / £9.

Try a selection of suitable chew toys:
http://www.ChinchillaBook.com/toys.htm (USA)
http://www.ChinchillaBook.com/toysuk.htm (UK)

Controversial Run-Around Balls

Many species of small companion animals can be placed in vented clear plastic "run-around" balls that provide them access to greater space and exercise while affording them a degree of protection.

The use of these balls with chinchillas is highly controversial, and would definitely qualify as a "supervision only" toy. The primary danger is that your pet will overheat inside the ball and succumb to heatstroke.

Never use a run-around ball with a chinchilla in temperatures greater than 70° F / 21° C and do not leave your pet inside for longer than 15 minutes.

Set a timer, and observe your pet closely. The risk of overheating is real and serious. Don't dismiss the potential.

The vents in the run-around ball are not sufficient to keep your chinchilla cool. The interior temperature of the ball will rise rapidly with the chin's physical exertion.

Dust Bath

A chinchilla should never be bathed in water. In the wild they use volcanic ash to keep their coats free of oil and debris.

When presented with a tray containing specially formulated chinchilla dust, they will happily engage in a frenzy of rolling that is, frankly, one of the cutest things your chin will do.

Always use a commercial dust for your chin. A product like Kaytee Chinchilla Dust Bath (2.5 lb / 1.13 kg) costs $10 / £6.

Many different kinds of trays can be used to hold the dust, which should not be deep. Judge according to the size of your tray, but typically just a few spoons' worth is more than enough.

(The dust bath process will be discussed in detail in the next chapter.)

Since chinchillas will make quite a mess when they roll around in their dust, a broad tray with sides is highly recommended.

It's also possible to find chinchilla bath "houses" that keep the whole process nicely contained.

Do not add clean dust on top of that which has been used. Throw out the used dust and start fresh at least every other bath.

Let your chinchilla enjoy a dust bath:
http://www.ChinchillaBook.com/dust.htm (USA)
http://www.ChinchillaBook.com/dustuk.htm (UK)

Comb

Chinchillas are never brushed, only combed. Select a stainless steel comb with moderately spaced teeth.

This will primarily be needed during those times when your chin is molting or shedding, roughly every 3 months.

Stainless steel combs for pets are available in a price range of $10-$15 / £6-£9.

Chinchilla Comb / Brush
http://www.ChinchillaBook.com/comb.htm (USA)
http://www.ChinchillaBook.com/combuk.htm (UK)

Small Pet Carrier

At any time that you must transport your chinchilla, your pet must be safely enclosed in a carrier. This may be necessary for trips to the vet, or even just as an expedient to corral your lively little chin while you clean its primary cage.

A small crate suitable for a dog or cat works fine, but it's best to try to get one that is made primarily of stainless steel as your chin will immediately start gnawing on plastic.

In order to find a travel crate in stainless steel (generally these are dog crates), budget about $50 / £31.

Estimated Total Set Up Costs

Cage
$175-$350 / £110-£220

Nest Box
$30 / £19

Bedding
2 cubic feet / 56.6 liters
$15 / £9

Litter Scoop
$5-$10 / £3-£6

Estimated Total Set Up Costs

Food Bowls
$20-$30 / £13-£19 for earthenware
$10-$15 / £6-£9 for stainless steel

Water Bottle
16-ounce / 0.5 liter
$18-$20 / £11-£13

Hay Rack
$8 / £5

Exercise Wheel
$25-$30 / £16-£19

Wooden Chewing Blocks
lots of 6-12
$12.50-$25 / £8-£16.

Dust Bath
2.5 lb / 1.13 kg - cost $10 / £6.

Stainless Steel Comb
$10-$15 / £6-£9.

Stainless Steel Travel Crate
$50 / £31

Total Estimated Cost:
$375 - $575
£235 - £360

Chapter 4 – Daily Chinchilla Care

Chinchillas are not especially high maintenance pets. They are easy to feed as long as there are no sudden changes in their diet. They do need a lot of room, and time out of their cages daily, but beyond that, you won't find life with your chin to be demanding.

Bringing Your Chinchilla Home

When you have fully established your pet's habitat, your next task is to make sure that there is at least one area in your house that is "chinchilla proof."

Understand that although you won't be letting your chin out of its cage for the first couple of weeks while it's settling in, going forward your pet will need time out to exercise every day.

Chinchilla Proofing

Select an area of your home that is easy to clean. Chinchillas cannot be litter trained or housebroken. They will do what they need to do whenever they need to do it. Fortunately, their droppings are dry and firm, and their urinary output is small.

Bathrooms and Hallways

Many chin parents pick a bathroom or hallway, although any area with tiled floors that can be easily closed off for a period of time will work.

If you do use a bathroom, make sure the toilet lid is down. A pet chinchilla can easily drown if it falls in.

Be sure to close all doors and windows. If your pet is really active, transport him to his play area in his carrier and take him back to his cage the same way.

An escaped chinchilla is VERY hard to catch, especially if they become frightened.

Secure All Chemicals and Plastics

In any room, there should be no access to any kind of chemicals. If cabinets are present, install child locks on the doors.

The same precaution extends to all varieties of houseplants, which should all be taken out of the area.

Don't give your chin access to any plastics on which they can gnaw, and beware of things like trash can liners that are a potential choking hazard.

Dangerous Cords and Cables

All electrical cords or cables including phone cords should be secured in cable minders. Chins are at a high risk for electrocution due to their constant chewing behavior.

Do not, however, underestimate a chin's ability to gnaw through anything. If you can use a room where there are no cords present at all, that is ideal.

Consider the Furniture

Anything that can be nibbled or chewed on should be removed or in some way protected — including the legs of tables and chairs.

Evaluate the space for any means of escape, or hiding. Remember that chinchillas are burrowing animals. They love to squeeze into very small spaces.

If you have your chin loose in the living room, beware of recliners and rockers. Chins can easily get inside and be seriously harmed or even killed by the mechanism.

Alternate Chewing Options

Offer your pet cardboard boxes during play time to help keep them interested. They can chew on those to their heart's content and hide in them as well.

Egg cartons are also a cheap chewing option, as are safe, non-treated wood blocks.

Be advised that if you don't give your chin something to chew on during play time, the little guy may just start gnawing on the nearest wall — and heaven help you if there's a stray bit of wallpaper!

Supervise Your Pet

No matter how "chinchilla proof" you believe the space to be, never leave your chin unsupervised. They can and do get themselves into all kinds of trouble because they are both exuberantly active and insatiably curious.

Play time should be one of your best bonding opportunities of the day. Don't just turn your chin loose and ignore him. Chinchillas are highly affectionate with their humans and enjoy interaction.

Talk to your pet and laugh at his antics. Often times if you show pleasure in something he's doing, your chin will repeat the action just to please you and to get more praise and affectionate approval.

Do an Eye-Level Check

One of the best ways to evaluate your success in chinchilla proofing a room is to get down to your chin's eye level and have a look around. You may see all kinds of interesting things you missed.

You can be certain, however, that your chin won't miss a thing, nor will he fail to investigate!

Getting Used to a New Home

Understand that moving to a new environment is very stressful for naturally timid and nervous animals like chinchillas. You will need to be patient and allow your pet time to adjust.

Be sure to drive straight home from the pet store or the breeder's facility to minimize the stress of travel for the chinchilla.

Covering the cage, or riding with it in the front wheel well or between the back seats is also a good choice. The chinchilla is not going to be watching the scenery roll by!

Leave Your Pet Alone at First

It's the most natural thing in the world to want to interact with a new pet, especially one as cute as a chinchilla, but it's important not to overwhelm the chin with attention at first.

He will need to get used to the sights, smells, and sounds of your home and to understand that his cage is his "safe place." It's really best not to try to handle your chin at all for the first few days.

An optimal method for introducing your chinchilla to its new home is to place the carrier inside the cage, open it, and let the chin emerge on its own.

Just put the carrier inside and leave – no matter how much you want to stay. You can observe from a safe distance, but it's best to leave the chinchilla alone for the first day.

Introduce Yourself Slowly

After the first 24 hours, you can introduce yourself to your new chin, but take it slowly and do things on your pet's terms.

Dim the lights in the room and let your chinchilla get a good look at you. Go into the room alone. It's best for a chin to bond completely with its primary caregiver before it meets any other members of the household.

If things seem to be going well, and the chin is not nervous, you can put your hand in the cage and very patiently wait for the chin to come to you and conduct a "sniff test."

Just stay still. If you like, hold out a small treat — perhaps a single raisin or a bit of carrot. Do not jerk your hand back if your chin gently nips your fingers while taking the treat. Do nothing to startle your pet.

If the chinchilla isn't interested in coming closer on day one, don't press the issue. Slowly and quietly withdraw your hand, leave the room, and try again the next day.

Ultimately Curiosity Takes Over

Ultimately, the chinchilla's curiosity will take over and your pet will come to you, and in time, even hop on your arm.

At that point, you can begin to lightly scratch its ears or face. At any time you sense fear, stop what you're doing and let your chin settle down.

Always use a soft, gentle voice. Chinchillas do not like loud noises. Your job is simply to be patient and slow. Earn your chin's trust.

After a couple of weeks, you'll likely be rewarded with a happy chirp when your pet sees you first thing in the day. By that time, you should be comfortable handling your chinchilla.

Handling Your Chinchilla

Not all chinchillas like being held, but it will be necessary to be able to pick up your pet. Always fully support your chin's body, bracing your pet with one hand under its backside.

Work up to handling with gradual sessions right outside the cage over a period of two weeks to a month. Try to get in about 20 minutes a day of sitting on the floor with your chin on your knee or in your lap.

Reinforce the behavior with small treats of oats, or one raisin cut in quarters. Don't let the chinchilla have the run of the room until you're sure you can safely retrieve it.

When holding your pet, keep the chinchilla snug against your chest. Don't dangle it out in front of you, as this will only scare the chin. Remember that chinchillas thrive on a sense of security.

Typically a chinchilla will sit near its owner in the beginning and enjoy being petted, but over time, you may well get your pet to let you cuddle it or invite it to sit in your lap for longer periods.

Understand, however, that young chinchillas are a force of nature and would much rather be rocketing off the walls than sitting placidly with you.

Nutrition for Your Chinchilla

Maintaining good nutrition for your chinchilla is the bedrock of solid care for your pet. Chins can be easily subject to digestive upsets, so it's important to get your pet on a good diet and keep him there.

Never make sudden dietary changes with a pet chinchilla. Diarrhea is a very serious condition for a chin and can be triggered easily. In the beginning, your pet should eat whatever it has been fed at the pet store or breeder's facility.

If you want to transition to another kind of food, or add better nutritional elements for your pet, do so very slowly.

Watch your pet's droppings. They should remain firm and dry at all times. If they are not, you're changing your chin's diet too rapidly.

Pellets, Your Pet's Staple Food

Commercially formulated chinchilla pellets will be the staple of your pet's diet. Typically a chin will eat about 2 tablespoons (U.S. or UK) daily, but there's no need to ration meals.

Pellets should be available to your chin at all times. Every few days throw out all the pellets in the bowl and start over with fresh food.

Do not feed your pet pellets that have been formulated for rabbits or any other species since malnutrition and liver damage can result. Always store your chin's pellets in a sealed container kept away from any source of moisture in a cool place out of the sun.

As a little extra treat, you can dust the pellets with rose hips powder available in your local health food store. This will make the meal sweeter for your chin, but won't add sugar to their nutritional profile.

In the United States, consider using Oxbow Chinchilla Deluxe pellets, which come in varying bags from 5 to 50 lbs. in a price range of $11 to $50.
In the UK, Charnwood Pellets are a favorite among enthusiasts. The company's "mature and maintenance" mixture is priced at £5.38 for 5 kgs.

Looking for Chinchilla food easily? Try:
http://www.ChinchillaBook.com/food.htm (USA)
http://www.ChinchillaBook.com/fooduk.htm (UK)

The Importance of Hay

A mix of good quality hays is essential to provide your chinchilla with adequate roughage and the dietary fiber it needs for optimum gastrointestinal health. Never let your chin run out of hay!

As a chinchilla chews hay, the grinding action also wears down its teeth, preventing both overgrowth and the development of dental spurs. Don't worry about your chin eating too much hay. That won't happen.

Remove the hay that has become scattered and soiled on a daily basis, and just keep replenishing the hay rack, which should be full at all times.

You'll know you have a good quality hay when it looks and smells clean and dry. Hay should not be dullish brown, nor should it be dusty or have a moldy smell. Also make sure the mixture does not have any thorns or burrs.

Pet chins will thrive on high fiber, low protein grass hays. The rationale for this is simple. Read the label on the pre-formulated pellets you're feeding your pet. In most cases, alfalfa will be a major ingredient. Alfalfa is both high fiber and high protein.

If your chin is getting the protein it needs from its pellet food, you don't want to add to that protein load in your choice of hay. For this reason the best options are:

- Timothy
- Mountain grass
- Brome
- Orchard grass

You can still give your chin a little alfalfa, maybe 2 or 3 times a week, because it is a good source of calcium, but don't overdo it.

If you are just introducing a rich hay like alfalfa, do so slowly to avoid gastrointestinal upset. (This is true of clover hay as well, which should also be used sparingly.)

Packaged timothy hay is available in a variety of sizes from 5-50 lbs. / 2.27-22.7 kg in a price range of $20-$65 / £12-£40.

What About Hay Cubes?

Hay cubes are compressed hay, generally timothy or alfalfa, that come packaged for purchase in pet stores. There are many instances where hay cubes are very convenient if your chin will eat them.

Cubes are perfect for travel, and they are not as messy as loose hay. It's a good idea to break the cube up into smaller chunks and to offer it to your chin in his food bowl.

Whether using loose hay or cubes, always make sure the material stays dry. If stored in a container, the receptacle should be vented to avoid the growth of mold and kept in a dry, cool place out of the sun.

Small, compressed "bales" of timothy hay are priced at $14 / £9 per 6 lb / 2.7 kg.

Treats for Your Chin

Be forewarned. Chinchillas are highly skilled beggars. They stand up on their hind legs, look at you imploringly, and often extend their little paws "asking."
It's adorable – and the great chinchilla con job. Don't fall for it! Chins like all sorts of things that simply are not good for them. Once a chin gets started on treats, there's no going back. He'll stuff himself and refuse his regular food.

Not only will you likely then be forced to battle obesity in your pet, but also wonky digestion. Nature designed chins to eat plant material filled with fiber, not fat, sugary treats or a lot of protein.

They have tiny little stomachs. They won't overeat on either their pellets or hay, but they will gorge themselves on treats. An imploring little chin may be hard to resist, but this is where tough love is called for on your part.

Under no circumstances should you ever give your chin anything containing any amount of chocolate, which can harm their digestion and their nervous system.
Also remove any corn in any pellet mix that is designated as a "treat." There are mixes available that contain dried fruit, vegetables, nuts, and seeds which you can use once or twice a week as a treat, dispensing no more than a teaspoon (U.S. or UK), but all corn should be picked out.

(Corn is highly subject to fungal content and the development of mold, which can cause bloat in your pet.)

You can use fresh or dried fruits as a treat 2 or 3 times a week in VERY small amounts (just a bite or two). Safe items on this list include:

- Banana
- Apple
- Grape
- Strawberry
- Apricot
- Cranberry
- Cherry
- Peach
- Raisin
- Prune
- Fig

Fruits and vegetables should never make up more than 10% of your chinchilla's total diet.

If you are training your chin to perform "tricks," or trying to reinforce positive behavior, pick items out of the treat mix to be used as rewards.

Alternately, you can also use oatmeal flakes from any standard oatmeal preparation. Use one flake at a time. You may think that's a miserly approach, but your chinchilla will just be happy to be getting something "extra."

Fresh Water

Your chinchilla's water bottle should be kept full and be clean at all times. In general, it's better to opt for a glass water bottle, as plastic may itself be toxic, or is subject to retaining bacteria.

Never wash your pet's water bottle with any chemical substance or soap. Give it a thorough scrubbing under hot water then allow it to cool before refilling it and returning it to the enclosure.

Use de-chlorinated water for your pet, or allow tap water to outgas for 24 hours before using it with your chinchilla.

Also, make sure the spout is placed at the level of your pet's mouth and not dripping.

A chinchilla's fur mats easily when it comes into contact with water, which is often a consequence of a faulty water bottle.

Grooming

Chinchillas should not be bathed in water, but must be provided with a dust bath in which they will happily roll to remove oil and debris from their coats.

Every other day, provide your chin with a dust bath in a large enough container for the little guy to roll freely. Use only specially formulated chinchilla dust.

Just a few spoons' worth is more than enough. There's no need to completely cover the bottom of the "bath." If possible, find a chinchilla bath "house" to contain the dust your pet will kick up.

Typically your chin will roll for 5-10 minutes, but if he's having a good time, just sit back and enjoy the show.

Generally it's best to present the chin with its dust bath outside of the habitat during free playtime.

Chinchilla dust is inexpensive, selling for about $6 / £4 per 3 lb / 1.4 kg.

Dust baths and occasional combing during heavy periods of shedding are the only aspects of chinchilla grooming you need to help with. A chinchilla's nails do not grow long, so trimming them is not needed.

Periodic Shedding

About every three months, your chinchilla will shed. Typically this process starts at the head and moves back toward the tail. Loose strands of hair will come out of the coat, so it's important to gently comb your pet, and to keep its cage clean and free of shed fur.

This process generally lasts about two weeks. The new hair pushes up through the old growth until a distinct line begins to appear. When the "priming line" reaches the tail, the shedding period is over.

Cage Maintenance

On a daily basis you should remove all soiled bedding from your chinchilla's habitat as well as fouled hay that has been scattered on the floor. Make sure your pet has fresh, clean food and water.

Each week you will want to completely change the bedding and wipe down the surfaces in the cage with a mixture of warm water and vinegar. Do not use harsh chemicals and make sure all surfaces are thoroughly rinsed and dry before you return your pet to its home.

At least once a month, completely disassemble and wash the cage, preferably taking it outside to be hosed down and dried in the sun.

Have an Emergency Plan

Since chinchillas are so susceptible to heat stress, it's important to have emergency supplies and a plan in place should you lose electricity during the hot months of the year.

If your air conditioning is not reliable even with the power on, you may want to consider purchasing a second window unit for the chinchilla room.

Using a thermometer, determine which room in the house is always the coolest. If you do not keep your pets there on a regular basis, be prepared to move them to this location during a power failure or on a very hot day.

Have heavy shades in place so you can dim the amount of sunlight entering the room, and use compact fluorescent or LED light bulbs that do not generate more heat.

Keep small marble tiles in the freezer so you can give your pets a cool place to sit. Pet stores sell tiles designed for this purpose or you can buy seconds and leftovers at tile and home improvement stores.

It's also a good idea to freeze water in glass jars or to use commercial cold packs. You don't want to put these inside the cage, but you can position them outside the cage to form a cool "wall."

Emergency battery packs that are available for $75 to $100 / £46 to £62 will give you enough power to run a small fan for several hours.

You won't want to direct the flow of air directly at your pets, but having a stream of air over ice packs or even wet towels can serve as a rudimentary air conditioner.

It is perfectly safe to give your chins a dish of ice to chew on. The ice won't hurt their teeth.

If conditions in the house get really bad, put your chinchillas in their travel cage, get them in the car with the AC on, and find an alternate location for them to spend the day.

Learning to Speak Chinchilla

Your chinchilla will communicate with you using a large vocabulary that is based on vocalization and body language.

Vocalizations

A chinchilla's loudest vocalization is a sort of guttural little "bark." It can have a range of meanings from grandstanding to look "big," to actual displeasure.

Whining is a step down from barking, indicating your pet wants something. If you listen closely, the sound of the request is evident.
Chinchillas only squeak when they're babies. An adult signals contentment and approval with a bleating coo or "chirp."

Nervous whimpering is just what you would imagine. "I don't like what's going on." Actual crying, however, is a sound filled with pain, and a very bad sign.

As prey animals, chinchillas do everything they can to not reveal that they are hurting. When they cry, the pain is severe and they need veterinary assistance.

Body Language

Chinchillas both smile and wink. When they do both, you're getting a really positive message. The winking is a quite conscious greeting. Wink back, or even put your face down near your chin's. You may be rewarded with a little kiss.

Chins also like to groom their people, often by grasping one of your fingers in their tiny hands and licking you. This is a huge compliment that signals their acceptance of your role in their herd or colony.

In addition to bouncing happily around their environment, chins will also stand up on their hind legs and do a kind of hopping dance, often in a circle. Since it's quite common for this to occur when music is playing, it's obvious the chins are enjoying themselves.

Rearing up on the hind legs can also indicate a defensive posture and may be a prelude to an incident of urine spraying, so make sure you're getting the message right.

If you think your chinchilla is unhappy about something, err on the side of caution and leave the little guy alone until he's calmed down.

Training Your Chinchilla?

With time and attention, almost all companion animals can either be taught tricks, or a native behavior can be reinforced so that it is executed on cue.

Clicker training is a good way to work with your chin, but you will want to modify the clicker so that its sound is barely audible. These devices are easy to find in pet stores and cost less than $5 / £3.

As an opening "lesson," watch for a behavior in your chin you like or that is cute or entertaining, like leaping from one perch to another.

When your chin makes the leap, click and reward your pet with a treat. Use single oat flakes to reinforce training routines so you don't get your chin started begging for things he shouldn't eat.
As soon as your clever little chinchilla realizes the click is associated with a treat, he will perform the behavior over and over again.

This sets the stage for you to direct "tricks," like having your pet run through a cardboard roll at a signal from the clicker.

Never scold a chinchilla. Simply reward correct or near correct behavior and ignore "failures." Chins are so anxious to please and interact with the human of their choice they will often repeat an action for no reason but that it got a laugh out of you.

Keep the training light, and always treat it as an aspect of play. Watch what your chinchilla does naturally, and build on those actions.

Chapter 5 - Health and Breeding

Chinchillas do not have many of the same health needs as more typical pets like cats and dogs. They do not, for instance, require vaccinations.

Most chinchilla owners report that their pets never have to go to the vet for more than their annual wellness check.

Spaying and neutering is not required unless you are housing a male and female pair and wish to avoid unwanted litters.

Deciding to Spay or Neuter

Opting to spay or neuter a chinchilla is a major decision that must be made in consultation with a qualified veterinarian.

The surgical procedures are highly delicate, and as discussed later in this chapter, there are concerns about the use of anesthesia with chinchillas.

Spaying a female chinchilla is far and away the more risky and complicated of the two procedures, and should not be considered unless there is an absolute medical necessity.

When trying to avoid unplanned litters in a male-female pair housed together, it is always better to have the male neutered.

The chances of a successful recovery without complications are much greater. The recuperation period will still be a week to ten days, during which time your pet may have to occupy separate quarters.

Note that in some cases with aggressive males, neutering is recommended to lower testosterone levels and to improve behavior. This is especially true in instances where males are housed together and one exhibits dominance.

An Initial Sick Spell

Typically chinchillas fall ill when they first go to a new home. The little animals will be suffering from stress and they may encounter some new bacteria or microbe to which they have no immunity.

This is especially true of young chinchillas whose immune systems are not fully developed, which is another reason to make sure young chins are fully weaned before they are adopted.

You can lessen the chances of an initial illness by feeding your new pet exactly the foods to which it is accustomed and taking all necessary measures to keep the animal calm and feeling safe.

In almost all cases, scrupulous husbandry is essential to good health. Chinchillas that live in clean, well-maintained habitats are hardy and happy.

Signs of Ill Health

You are always your pet's best health insurance. The longer you live with your chinchilla, the more you will understand what is "normal" for your pet. If you have the sense that something is wrong, it probably is.

Never hesitate to seek the advice and help of your veterinarian for fear of looking like an over-protective chin parent. Remember that chinchillas are prey animals. They will do everything they can not to appear sick because hiding illness is part of their survival instinct.

Although normally quite healthy, chinchillas are subject to gastrointestinal upsets that must be addressed quickly. They can also develop serious dental problems that impair their ability to eat.

A vigilant owner on the watch for any signs of trouble is the foundation of good pet healthcare. Things to watch for include:

- A lack of appetite or a dramatically reduced appetite.

- Any difficulty eating as in labored or painful chewing or drooling.

- Changes in stools, which should normally be dry and firm.

- Teeth grinding, or other indications of the teeth being overgrown.

- Any lumps or lesions on the body.

- Dry and flaking skin.

- Difficulty urinating or decreased urine output.

- Discharge from the mouth or eyes.

- Labored breathing.

- Apparent lameness or limping as well as weakness or loss of agility.

- Any tenderness, especially of the abdomen when handling.

Also be aware of any neurological symptoms like trembling, paralysis, or something like a drooping eye.

Common Illnesses and Concerns

The following conditions are those most commonly seen in pet chinchillas. This is not, however, a comprehensive compendium and is not intended as a substitute for a veterinary consultation when your pet is showing signs of ill health.

Bites and Lacerations

When chinchillas, especially males, are housed together, bite wounds are fairly common. In many instances chins are also bitten by other animals present in the household.

In either case, the wounds can become infected as chins are somewhat susceptible to abscesses. These infections spread rapidly in the body and are often fatal.

Any time that your chinchilla suffers any kind of open wound, bite, or laceration, the timely intervention of a veterinarian is essential.

Chinchillas and Antibiotics

Typically in an instance of an open wound, a vet's response will be to prescribe an antibiotic. You must make certain that your vet has experience with this species. Don't just assume on this point — ask, and be persistent.

The balance of microorganisms in the chinchilla's digestive system is complex and can be destroyed by the administration of antibiotics. This, in turn, can lead to the overgrowth of potentially deadly bacteria.

With chinchillas, it's important to avoid:

- Penicillins
- Cephalosporins
- Clindamycin
- Lincomycin
- Erythromycins

Broken Bones

A broken bone is an emergency requiring immediate attention. Generally the cause is some element of the chin's housing that has allowed your pet's foot to get caught.

For fractures that are caught when they are new, the veterinarian will use a standard splint or cast. In some cases it may even be necessary to pin the bone.

Since chinchillas are very bad to gnaw at casts or bandages, the vet will outfit your pet with a cone-shaped collar so it can't reach the affected area to chew.

Typically, broken bones in chinchillas heal in about three weeks. Your pet's activities will need to be restricted for the next few weeks, however.

If the fracture has gone undetected, it is not uncommon for amputation to be required. Chinchillas tolerate this procedure quite well, with no serious loss of mobility.

The Slobbers

This is a dental condition in which the teeth are overgrown and/or sharp edges have formed on the incisors or molars. The condition derives its name from the fact that the discomfort and inability to chew often leads to drooling. Other marked symptoms include weight loss, and tearing of the eyes on the side where the affected tooth or teeth are located. An oral examination is required to determine the exact state of the mouth.

The chinchilla will need to be sedated as X-rays may also be required. The teeth will have to be trimmed, and again antibiotics may be indicated.

If the elongation is caused by an overgrowth of the roots, the condition is more serious and may be irreversible.

Chinchillas and Anesthesia

Chinchillas, as a rule, do not tolerate anesthesia well. Your vet should be experienced in administering anesthesia to chins, or should consult with a vet who has done so.

The recommended anesthesia for chins are isoflurane and sevoflurane because the animals wake up very quickly.

Be sure that your vet is also aware of the tendency of chinchillas to become easily dehydrated as subcutaneous fluid supplementation may be indicated.

Diarrhea

Any alteration in the consistency of your pet's droppings must be treated promptly. If you have made a change to your chinchilla's diet, remove the new food or dramatically cut back on the amount being given. It can also help to offer your chin small pieces of dry toast.

Chinchillas have specialized digestive systems with an intervening sac at the juncture point of the small and large intestines called the "cecum." The bacteria and protozoa that are present in this organ are crucial to digestion.

Often digestive ailments can be traced to a disruption in the pH level in the cecum and will resolve when diet is stabilized. If no improvement is evident within a few hours, however, seek veterinarian treatment.

If your pet has parasites, a deworming agent is indicated. Bacterial infections will require antibiotics.

NEVER use over-the-counter medications with your pet for any reason unless instructed to do so by a qualified veterinarian.

Constipation

On the opposite end of the spectrum, chins can also suffer from constipation if they have too much protein in their diets or if they are stressed. Their stools become hard and are quite small.

Typical remedies include a raisin, some prune juice, or a feline hairball remedy. If the stools do not soften, or if your chinchilla is in pain when defecating, contact the vet immediately.

Gas or Bloat

When chinchillas are fed fresh grass, greens, or any food with too much sugar, they will develop a painful case of gas. For this reason, these foods should never be part of your pet's diet.

If your chinchilla is suffering from gas, it will burp or be flatulent as the body attempts to release the pressure.

Remove your pet's food for a day and encourage the chinchilla to exercise.

If the stomach is distended or feels spongy or "doughy" to the touch, your pet is bloated and will need immediate veterinary attention.

Heat Stroke

Heat stroke is an emergency condition in chinchillas that must be immediately addressed or death may result. If you find your chinchilla stretched out with labored breathing, immediately remove the animal to a cooler area.

Turn a fan on in the room, but do not allow the air to blow directly on your chin. Gently apply a cool cloth to the armpits, groin, and neck to help lower body temperature.

The best "treatment" for heat stroke is prevention. Never place your chin's enclosure in front of a window, and vigilantly monitor the temperature in the surrounding area, using fans for air circulation if necessary.
Strive for a temperature of 75° F / 24° C or less. Chins tolerate cooler temperatures much better than heat. After all, they are wearing thick fur coats!

Fur Chewing

If you see evidence of fur chewing in chinchillas housed together, first separate the pair to determine if the damage is self-inflicted or if the cage mate is responsible.

Overcrowding is often at the root of this particular problem, especially if a new chinchilla has just been introduced to the habitat.

Other environmental causes of fur chewing include sleep deprivation (often from too much light) and any loud noises that are frightening your pet and causing it to be anxious.

When stress is the cause, it can take some time for the fur to regrow and, unfortunately, the behavior can become habitual.

It's important to do everything you can to make your chinchilla feel more secure, including buying a larger habitat and increasing the available hiding and sleeping places.

Since it is extremely rare for chinchillas to be afflicted with parasites that attack the skin and coat, fur chewing can almost always be traced to an environmental issue.
Very rarely if your pet is not getting enough fiber, it may take to eating odd substances — including its own fur — to compensate, a condition called "pica."

Skin irritation from a change in bedding is also a potential problem, but if you stick with aspen shavings rather than pine or cedar, this should not be an issue.

Parasites

Chinchillas are not troubled with external parasites like fleas, ticks, and mites because their coats are simply too dense for the "bugs" to get down to the skin where they would normally feed on blood.

Chinchillas can, however, be subject to internal parasites that attack the gastrointestinal tract including, but not limited to:

- Giardia
- Coccidian
- Cryptosporidia
- Tapeworms
- Hookworms
- Nematodes
- Roundworms
- Pinworms

All are treatable, but your veterinarian will need to analyze a fresh stool sample in order to determine the correct treatment.

Caring for Older Chinchillas

Since chinchillas can live to 20 years of age, you will, at some point, have a senior citizen on your hands. Typically older chins become less active, and it may be necessary to redesign their habitat so they can climb more easily.

Since older chins are less able to regulate their body temperature, make sure the ambient temperature stays constant in the room where they are housed.

Cataracts are common in older chinchillas and are evident as a milky, opaque coating on the eyes. This condition is not typically treated, and other than contributing to some diminishment of activity, is well tolerated by chinchillas.

Extra vigilance in monitoring tooth growth is also essential in older chins, and it's important to check the color of the teeth. If excessive yellowing is visible, your pet's kidney function should be evaluated.

Breeding

Typically it is recommended that pet owners not breed their chinchillas as there are far too many unwanted chins already. Since pet stores frequently misidentify gender, unplanned pregnancies do occur fairly often in chinchillas kept in pairs.

Chins become sexually mature at age 4-6 months. In most cases you will not know that your pets have mated until you find a deposit of white material in the cage referred to as a "copulatory plug." This indicates that in about 111 days, you will be a chin grandparent.

When you are sure that mating has occurred, immediately separate the pair and let the female have her young on her own. Keep the pair separated in the future or consider having one or both of your pets neutered.

Chinchilla females give birth to 1-4 "kits" that will be born over a period of 2-3 hours at night. The babies will be fully developed at birth, and should remain with their mother for 8-16 weeks or until they are completely weaned.

A baby chinchilla's dietary requirements are the same as those of an adult once they are ready for solid food.

Vet Visits

When it is necessary to take your chinchilla to the vet, always transport your pet in a secure carrier and never, under any circumstances, leave the chin unattended in a vehicle.

Keep the air conditioning on during the trip to avoid stressing your pet more due to changes in its environmental temperature.

If the visit is taking place during hot weather, start the car and let the air run until the internal temperature cools down to match that of your home.

Drive with the carrier in the front foot well or between the rear seats. The less your chin can see of what's going on around it, the more it will feel it's in a secure "cave."

At the clinic, hold the carrier in your lap. Do not set it on the ground. Your chinchilla will be frightened of other animals in the waiting room. If necessary, cover the carrier to give your pet a greater sense of security and sit in the quietest area you can find.

Afterword

Hopefully you now have enough information to decide if keeping a chinchilla as a pet is right for you. While not a particularly demanding animal, chins do have very definite needs in terms of habitat and environment that will be your responsibility to fulfill.

Long before you ever bring your chinchilla home from the pet store or the breeder, you should have acquired your new pet's cage and outfitted it with all the "decorations" that will make the habitat your chinchilla's burrow.

Additionally, you should select an area in your home where your chin can be out of its cage — with supervision — and play safe of all the environmental hazards that can imperil its life.

Be prepared to spend part of each evening with your chinchilla allowing it to get its exercise and to strengthen the bond of trust you will start building on day one.

Make no mistake, chinchillas do take some patience in the beginning. They are timid and nervous creatures, approaching the world from the perspective of a prey animal.

They are, essentially, always waiting for something to attack and eat them because in the wild, that's exactly what can and does happen to them! The safer your chinchilla feels with you in your home, the happier and healthier it will be.

Chins are highly intelligent, and your pet will soon come to recognize you, often greeting you with a happy little chirp. With a potential lifespan of 20 years, you and your pet will come to know one another quite well with the passing of time.

Overall, chinchillas are hardy pets, with only a few health conditions to which they may be subject. Gastrointestinal upsets and dental care top that list. Both are completely manageable with scrupulous husbandry and the assistance of a qualified veterinarian.

While once prized – and exploited for their fur – chinchillas are now beloved for their excellent qualities as companion animals. Clean, quiet, and truly adorable, a chin can be an excellent addition to your life and household.

Relevant Websites

Mutation Chinchilla Breeder Association
http://www.mutationchinchilla.com

Common Diseases of Pet Chinchillas
http://www.beckeranimalhospital.com/2011/12/common-diseases-of-pet-chinchillas

Chinchilla Basics
http://www.heidihoefer.com/pages/sm_mammals/chinchilla_basics.htm

Chinchilla Care
http://www.allcreaturesah.com/Chinchilla%20Care.pdf

The Chinchilla Club
http://www.chinclub.net

Pet Chinchilla: To Have or Not to Have
http://www.cutehomepets.com/pet-chinchilla-to-have-or-not-to-have

Chin Care
http://www.chincare.com

Before You Get a Chinchilla
owningchinchillas.webs.com/before-you-get-a-chinchilla

Relevant Websites

Chinchilla World
http://www.chinchillaworld.com

Chinchilla Chronicles
http://www.chinchillachronicles.com

Frequently Asked Questions

Although reading the full text will give you the detailed understanding required to keep chinchillas as pets, the following are some of the most frequently asked questions about these active and adorable creatures.

Where do chinchillas live in the wild?

Europeans first became aware of chinchillas when Spanish explorers saw them in the Andes Mountains of South America. The little creatures, hunted as food and for their fur, were named for the Chincha Indians. Today, chinchillas are protected from hunters and are bred widely in captivity as pets.

Do chinchillas live a long time?

Yes, the life span of a chinchilla is 15-20 years, so if you adopt one, it will be with you a good while. Be prepared for that fact in advance!

Are chinchillas big?

When a chinchilla is fully grown it will be about 12 in (30 cm) long and weigh 18-25 oz (510-709 g). Usually, females are larger, but size tends to vary rather widely by individual.

Are chinchillas expensive?

Prices vary widely depending on where you are buying your pet. From a breeder, prices typically fall in the $50-$80 / £30-£50 range, while a pet store may charge as much as $125 / £78.

The more exotic color variations or those animals that are rated as "show" quality may cost significantly more.

Should I get one chinchilla or two?

If you have a single chinchilla for a pet, be prepared to give it lots of attention and intellectual stimulation. If you have the room, and are willing to put in the effort, pairs of same gender chinchillas will live happily together in most cases after an initial period of getting to know one another.

What should I feed my chinchilla?

You can purchase commercial chinchilla food pellets, but your pet will also need grass hay and lots of fresh water. For treats, you can feed your "chin" raisins or little bits of fresh fruit.

Be careful, though. Chinchillas love all kinds of things that aren't good for them, like ice cream. If you let your pet get used to "goodies" all the time, he'll likely refuse to eat his regular food. Chinchillas can be quite stubborn!

What kind of cage should I buy to house my chinchilla?

With this species, it's best to think "up" and opt for a vertical cage. Chins love to jump and climb, so they will love a habitat with solid ramps, platforms, and perches. Make sure they have a square of floor space that measures 2 ft x 2 ft (0.6 m x 0.6 m).

Cages with wire bottoms are not recommended unless you provide your pet with cushioned seating areas. Wire mesh cages can cause significant problems with your chinchilla's feet.

So do chinchillas just sit in their cages?

Hardly! A pet chinchilla needs and wants a lot of your time and attention every day. You'll need to spend some time "chin proofing" part of your home and learning to interact with your chin in ways it enjoys. They really don't make great pets for young children because many don't like to be held and cuddled.

They are, however, really curious by nature and born investigators. This trait can lead them to get into all kinds of trouble, so they should never be left out of the cage unsupervised.

What kind of things will a chinchilla need inside its cage?

In terms of cage structure, you'll want lots of platforms and shelves so your pet can jump and climb. A cardboard or wooden box makes a perfect nest box. Chinchillas prefer their own little "cave" for sleeping and hiding. Line the bottom of the box with wood shavings.

You'll also need a glass water bottle with a "lixit" tip, an exercise wheel, some toys, a food bowl that can attach to the side of the cage, and a hay rack.

Chinchillas play with toys?

You bet they do! And these little guys chew a lot, so make sure they have things to keep themselves occupied. If they don't, they'll chew on just about anything they can find, and wreak all kinds of havoc in your home.

In addition to wooden toys (untreated and free of toxic dyes), include some branches in your chin's habitat for gnawing. Apple branches that are insecticide free are an excellent choice.

Chinchillas also enjoy scampering up and down solid ramps, and going in and out of tunnels. Basically think of the habitat in terms of an "obstacle course" and "decorate" accordingly.

What do I need to do to "chinchilla proof?"

Never underestimate just how curious and inquisitive a chinchilla can be. They will often check something out by biting it. They're trying to determine if the object is edible, but if they bite into something dangerous, like an electrical cord, the results can be tragic.

You'll need to encase all cords in the room in cord minders and get rid of any potential choking hazards. Also remove all plastics and any potentially toxic substance.

If the room has cabinets in which dangerous items are stored, use child safety locks to keep your chin out. Also make sure they can't get close to any source of heat, or any container of water in which they could drown.

It's a good idea to get down on the floor at chinchilla eye level and survey everything as if you were a curious chinchilla on a mission.

Remove all hazards and get anything out of the room that's unsafe for your pet to chew on, or that you don't want destroyed. Consider wrapping the legs of wooden tables, and don't even think about leaving books out!

I've just brought my chinchilla home. I'm trying to make friends with it. Any advice?

Patience. If you have a young chinchilla that hasn't been socialized much, it can take a while for the little guy to get used to you. Some chins really aren't that fond of being held, but this varies by individual, so don't give up. Just take things slow and don't do anything to overwhelm your pet.

For the first few days, just let the chinchilla smell your hand. Let the animal come to you. Ultimately his curiosity will get the better of him and he'll jump up on your arm.

Typically within a couple of weeks, chinchillas come to regard their new cage as a safe base and develop a bond of trust with their human.

Typically it's best not to let your chinchilla play outside of its cage until you're sure you can handle it and retrieve the animal at the end of play time without a struggle.

Chinchillas are fast, and when they're frightened, they can get away from you in an instant.

What's the right way to hold a chinchilla?

Hold your pet securely against your body supporting it completely at all times. Chinchillas do not like to be held in mid-air, which is frightening to them. Never pick your pet up by the tail, or grab the tail in an effort to stop an escape.

Sometimes when I'm holding my pet and it squirms away, some fur comes out. Why?

This is a defense mechanism. The hair turns loose so the chinchilla can't be restrained that way. It's perfectly normal, but hopefully this will only occur if your pet becomes startled in some way. Once your chinchilla knows and trusts you, it really shouldn't struggle to get away.

Can I use a harness with my chinchilla?

No. A chinchilla's skeletal structure is too fragile to make it safe to use a harness and lead with these animals the way you would with a rabbit.

Do chinchillas have a favorite time of day to play?

Yes, chinchillas are nocturnal. During the day, your chin will sleep most of the time. These little guys like routine, so don't wake him up. Typically your pet will be much more active and desirous of your attention in the evenings.

Do I need to bathe my chinchilla?

No. Instead of bathing your chinchilla, provide it with a ceramic bowl filled with about 2 in / 5 cm of dust. Dust "baths" will keep your pet's coat and skin in excellent shape, removing both oil and dirt from the fur.

You can purchase commercial dust online or in a pet store to use for this purpose. Typically chinchillas will spend anywhere from 20 minutes to an hour rolling happily in their dust baths several times a week.

What is involved in cleaning up my chinchilla's cage?

You'll have both daily and weekly maintenance chores in regard to your chinchilla's habitat. Every day you'll need to remove soiled bedding and check all the accessories for chewing damage that might lead to a choking hazard.

Expect to replace items regularly in the habitat for this reason. Obviously your pet will need fresh food and water every day.

On a weekly basis, plan on completely disinfecting your chin's cage. If the unit has a pan for droppings, wash it with vinegar and water and let it air dry in the sun. Wash all of your pet's accessories and toys and completely replace all of the bedding material.

What's the most important aspect of chinchilla health care?

Looking after your pet's dental health. Chinchillas have open-rooted teeth that will continue to grow throughout your pet's life at a rate of roughly 2-3 in (5-8 cm) annually.

In order to keep the teeth worn down so they do not inhibit the chinchilla's ability to eat, you must provide plenty of chew toys.

Appendix 1 – Chinchilla Breeders

USA

Alabama

Cheryl's Little Angels
6351 Covington Lane
Tuscaloosa, AL 35405
http://www.cherylslittleangels.com/Connecticut

Arizona

Fur-Ever Chins
http://www.fur-everchins.com

California

Chinchilla Amore Formerly 4Everchins
Orangevale, CA 95662
Phone: 916-412-4332

Diamond Blue [1408]
Salinas, CA 93907
Napplepie@aol.com

Chinchilla Chateau
Manteca, CA 95336
chinchillachateau@gmail.com

RDZC Ranch
Ridgecrest, CA 93555
Phone: 714-745-0484

Cuddle Bug Chinchillas
Riverside, CA 92506
951-784-4195
cuddlebug.dyndns.org

Chiniverse
Sacramento, CA 95817
916-296-6043

Nancy Gao's Chinchillas [1401]
Pasadena, CA 91030
626-991-7772

Ridge Chinchillas [1308]
Paradise, CA 95969
530-520-6524w
http://www.qualitymutationchinchillas.com

Colorado

Mt. View Chinchilla Ranch
Ft. Collins, CO 80524
970-482-1834

Silver Spruce Chinchillas
Crawford, CO 81415
970-921-7231

Connecticut

Poetrue's Pets
East Hartford, CT
poetruespets@hotmail.com

Delaware

Angel's Chinchillas
http://www.angelschins.chinchillas.org/

Florida

Blue Ribbon Chinchillas
Clermont, FL 34711
http://www.blueribbonchinchillas.com

Lyn's Chins, Etc.
Orlando, FL 32803
http://www.centralfloridachinchillas.com

Georgia

Big Daddy Chinchillas
Locust Grove, GA 30248
http://www.bigdaddyschinchillas.com

Gold Heart Chinchillas
Flowery Heart, Georgia
http://www.goldheartchinchillas.com

Hawaii

Chinchilla Villas
http://www.chinchillavillas.com

Illinois

Starved Rock Chinchillas
Utica, IL 61373
815-667-4728

Indiana

Chinchillas By Design
Nappanee, IN 46550
http://www.chinchillasbydesign.net

Kansas

M&C Chins
Burlington, KS
mcchins@hotmail.com

Maryland

Sycamore Chins
Odenton, MD 21113-2297
410-695-0194

Michigan

Becky's Chinchillas
Six Lakes, MI 48886
becky@beckyschinchillas.com

JAGS Chinchillas
Houghton Lake, MI 48629
http://www.jagschinchillas.com

Maine

SydChilla Chinchilla
Augusta, ME 04330
http://www.sydchilla.com

Massachusetts

Cape Cod Chinchillas
Brewster, MA
508-364-6287

J and J Chinchillas
http://www.jandjchinchillas.webs.com/

Minnesota

Dan and Ann Harris
Fairmont, MN 56031
507-238-1177

Moulton Chinchilla Ranch
Rochester, MN 55902
507-288-6334

Missouri

Kansas City Chinchillas
Kansas City, MO 64912
816-547-8712
kansas.city.chinchillas.org

Nancy McConke
St. Louis, MO 63128
314-200-6185

Merritt Chinchilla Ranch
Napolean, MO 64074
816-934-2513

New Jersey

Mt Zion Chinchillas
Hillsborough, NJ 08844
809-466-0906

New York

Kuby Kritters
Akron, NY 14004
716-908-4745

Godin's Chinchillas
Glenville, NY
518-368-1019

North Carolina

Critter Cages NC
Asheboro, NC 27205
336-403-3296

Ohio

JT&C Chins
Akron, OH 44310
330-205-4634 (Jim)
330-289-7669 (Coty

Hummel Chinchillas
Shelby, OH 44875
419-347-6790

Ryerson Chinchillas
Plymouth, OH 44865
http://www.ryersonchinchilla.com

Ritterspach Chinchilla
Jenera, OH 45841
http://www.chinchillas.com

Royal Oaks Chinchilla Ranch
Plymouth, OH 44865
419-687-8362

Ralph & Barbara Shoots
Westerville, OH 43081
614-855-1762

Pennsylvania

Chincherub
Downingtown, PA 19335
http://www.chincherub.chinchillas.org

Chinvet
Carnegie, PA 15106
412-279-4649

Silkrhein Chins
Loretto, PA 15940
814-934-7177

Texas

Chinny Chin Chins Unlimited
Amarillo, TX 79118-8923
806-622-9473

South Carolina

Ann Ingram
4370 Wood Forest Drive
Rock Hill, SC 29732
903-327-2877

Vermont

D.J.'s Chinchilla Ranch
Orwell, VT 05760-9793
802-948-2886

Washington

Viking Chinchilla
22204 NE 25th Way
Sammamish, WA
http://www.viking-chinchillas.com

Wisconsin

B&B Chinchillas
Dodgeville, WI 53533
http://www.bbchinchillas.com

Appendix 1 – Chinchilla Breeders

UK

Etherdale Chinchillas
http://www.edchinchillas.co.uk/

Greenwood Chinchillas
http://www.greenwoodchinchillas.co.uk/

Davidson Chinchillas
http://www.davidson-chinchillas.co.uk/

Granite City Chinchillas
http://www.granitecitychinchillas.co.uk/

Elm Chinchillas
http://www.elmchins.co.uk/

Azure Chinchillas
http://www.azure-chinchillas.co.uk/

Merlin Chinchillas
http://www.merlin.chinchillas.org/

Nebula and Friends
http://www.nebulaandfriends.atspace.com/

Appendix 2 Rescue Organizations

USA

California

http://www.chinchillarescue.org
http://www.freewebs.com/ilovechinschinchillas/index.htm

Connecticut

http://www.foreverfeistychinchilla.org

Florida

http://www.freewebs.com/crazy_chinnie/
http://www.orgsites.com/fl/thechinranch1/

Louisiana

http://www.freewebs.com/nolachinrescue/

Ohio

http://www.forchinatechins.com/

http://www.sewardbreeders.com/

Vermont

http://www.malley.chinchillas.org/

Virginia

http://www.whimsys-menagerie.com/

UK

http://www.chinchillas2home.co.uk/

http://www.freewebs.com/brunelchins/rescuedchins.htm

http://www.chinchillas4life.co.uk/

Glossary

A

Agouti - The name that describes the alternating bands of light and dark coloration in the fur of a chinchilla.

B

Bedding - Any material used in the bottom of your chinchilla's cage is referred to as bedding. The favored material is aspen shavings. Do not use either pine or cedar shavings. Both contain strong phenols that may lead to skin, coat, respiratory, and liver problems.

C

Cage - Pet chinchillas are typically kept in cages as their primary habitat. The best selection is a tall cage with few plastic parts since chinchillas chew vigorously. The cage should include features to allow for jumping and climbing like shelves, solid ramps, and platforms.

Caviomorph - A group of rodents that includes guinea pigs and chinchillas.

Cecum - The cecum is an enlarged portion of the chinchilla's digestive tract between the small and large intestine. Beneficial bacteria in the cecum aids in breaking down ingested plant material.

Chew toys - It is absolutely essentially to provide your chinchilla with safe toys for chewing. Hard wood items that do not contain dyes and that have not been exposed to insecticides and chemicals are the best choices. Avoid hard plastics as your pet may swallow the fragments. Chew toys are necessary for proper dental health.

Chin - Enthusiasts use the nickname "chin" quite often to refer to their pets.

Chinchilla proof - This is the process of making a room or an area safe for a chinchilla to spend time out of its cage. Since chinchillas chew so vigorously, it's important to secure all potential hazards like electrical cords, and to make sure your pet does not have access to toxic substances. It might also be a good idea to wrap wooden furniture legs.

Colony - The appropriate term for chinchillas living together in a group.

Cord minders - Cord minders or covers are generally tubes or covers into which electrical cards are channeled to keep a pet like a chinchilla from chewing the wires. Using cord minders is an important part of securing a room as "chinchilla proof."

D

Dust bath - Rather than bathing in water, chinchillas prefer to roll in dust to clean oil and dirt out of their fur. Many chins will spend 20 minutes to an hour in their dust bath daily. Special dust for this purpose is available online or in pet stores.

G

Gestation - The period of time that elapses between conception and birth.

H

Heatstroke - Chinchillas are especially vulnerable to heat stroke, a dangerous physical condition caused by an environment that is overly hot.

I

Incisors - In chinchillas, the incisors are the two long front teeth that are located in the center of both the top and bottom jaw.

K

Kit - The proper term for a baby chinchilla.

L

Lactation - That period during which a female chinchilla is producing milk for the nourishment of her young.

M

Malocclusion - An inherited or accidental condition in which there is a deviation in the alignment of the incisor teeth that may cause there to be a need for the teeth to be trimmed so the chinchilla can eat properly.

N

Nest box - A wooden or cardboard box in which your chinchilla will sleep or hide. Line the nest box with aspen wood shavings, but do not use pine or cedar. Both are toxic to your pet.

Nocturnal - Animals that are most active at night and that sleep during the day are said to be nocturnal.

Index

Suggestions / Reviews

I really hope you liked the book and found it useful.

A LOT of time and hard work went into writing it. I have loved chinchillas for years and thought it was about time I put some knowledge down on paper for others to use.

Almost certainly you purchased this book online so I'm sure you'll be contacted soon asking for your review of it by the book seller you ordered it through. I would be very, very grateful if you could provide a positive review please.

However if you are unhappy with the book or feel I have left out information then please do get in contact first (before leaving the review) and hopefully I can help.

I'm happy to rewrite / add sections if you feel it would improve the book for other readers in the future. Simply email me at:

thomas@chinchillabook.com

with your suggestions and I'll get back to you as soon as I can (it may take a few days). If I can I will then act on your ideas and revise the book and send you a free copy (and others who joined our free club via http://www.chinchillabook.com) with the updated book ASAP just as a 'thank you' for helping to improve it.

Thank you again

Thomas Layton

Made in United States
North Haven, CT
09 November 2021